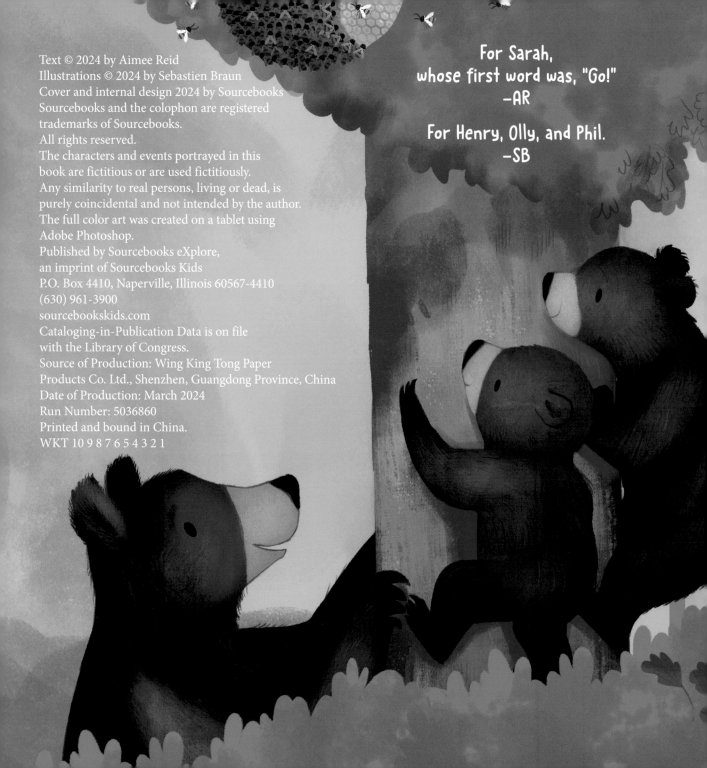

Text © 2024 by Aimee Reid
Illustrations © 2024 by Sebastien Braun
Cover and internal design 2024 by Sourcebooks
Sourcebooks and the colophon are registered
trademarks of Sourcebooks.
All rights reserved.
The characters and events portrayed in this
book are fictitious or are used fictitiously.
Any similarity to real persons, living or dead, is
purely coincidental and not intended by the author.
The full color art was created on a tablet using
Adobe Photoshop.
Published by Sourcebooks eXplore,
an imprint of Sourcebooks Kids
P.O. Box 4410, Naperville, Illinois 60567-4410
(630) 961-3900
sourcebookskids.com
Cataloging-in-Publication Data is on file
with the Library of Congress.
Source of Production: Wing King Tong Paper
Products Co. Ltd., Shenzhen, Guangdong Province, China
Date of Production: March 2024
Run Number: 5036860
Printed and bound in China.
WKT 10 9 8 7 6 5 4 3 2 1

For Sarah,
whose first word was, "Go!"
—AR

For Henry, Olly, and Phil.
—SB

BABY ANIMALS TRYING

A Celebration of First Moments

Words by Aimee Reid   Pictures by Sebastien Braun

sourcebooks
eXplore

Greeting the morning through eager, new eyes.

Baby rabbits open their eyes after about ten days.

Peacefully gliding beneath moonlit skies.

For the first couple of weeks, loons carry their babies on their backs on the water.

Joining together to howl with the pack.

At three to four weeks, wolf cubs begin to howl with their families.

Reaching to gather a tasty, new snack.

Young elephants must learn to work their trunks before using them to choose treats.

Rising on shaky legs, learning to stand.

Foals stand up within an hour of being born.

Tumbling and playing on wide-open land.

After about six weeks, lion cubs start to
pounce and tussle with their siblings.

Running to see just how fast you can go.

Giraffes begin to walk, lope, and jog about an hour after birth.

Slipping with speed down a slide made of snow.

Baby seals pull themselves forward by using their front flippers.

Climbing for honey that's fresh from the hive.

At three or four months, black bears start to scale trees.

Braving the water and daring to dive.

River otters learn to swim at about four
weeks and can dive at around ten weeks.

Swinging and swirling beneath a tall tree.

Young orangutans use vines and branches
to move through the trees.

Calling to hear your voice call back to me.

Baby beluga whales learn to make special calls to their mothers within one to two years after birth.

I'll be beside you wherever you go.

Human children learn to walk after several months.

Cheering with wonder and joy...

...as you grow.

ANIMAL MILESTONES

Rabbits

Baby rabbits first leave the nest around three to five weeks after birth. They will be about as big as a chipmunk by this age and are able to hop. Their mothers will still feed them until they can live on their own.

Loons

Loon chicks enter the water on their first day of life! Because their swimming muscles need to grow stronger, they will ride on their parents' backs for about two weeks.

Wolves

By the time wolf pups are four months old, they regularly howl with their pack. Wolves do this to communicate with each other, and they howl more if they are separated from another wolf they are close with.

Elephants

An elephant trunk is a combination of its nose and upper lip. Young calves must practice working their trunk muscles to grip objects, drink, and eat. Once this skill is mastered, they can pick up objects as small as a grain of rice.

Horses

A foal begins trying to stand right after it is born. When it can stay upright on its feet, it will begin to nurse from its mother. A foal's legs are almost full length at birth, which means it can keep up when the herd is on the move.

Lions

Lionesses often have about three or more cubs at a time. Cubs play together, jumping on each other's backs or mouthing one another's necks. Playing is an essential way for cubs to make connections to the other lions in the pride.

Giraffes

Both adult and young giraffes have longer front legs than back legs. A baby giraffe must learn to make its legs work in two different ways. When walking, its left legs move together, and then its right legs move together. When it runs, its back legs move together, crossing outside and in front of its front legs.

Harp Seals

Harp seals have two sets of flippers. Their front set can rotate and has big claws. The back set has smaller claws. These flippers help them move forward much like a caterpillar does. Sometimes seals slip and slide on the snow!

Black Bears

Before they are even six months old, black bears are terrific climbers. Their curved claws help them cling well to trees. They grip with their front legs and use their back legs to push themselves up. A small black bear can climb fast, reaching the top of a tall tree in several seconds.

River Otters

River otters need to take swimming lessons from their mothers. A mother otter grasps her baby by the neck and guides it into the water. She holds her pup while she dives and swims back to the surface, repeating the lesson until the pup can swim on its own.

Orangutans

Orangutans have four fingers and an opposable thumb, like human hands. They also have four long toes and an opposable toe. Curved hands and feet make it easy for them to grip vines and branches, and they spend most of their time in trees. By one year of age, most orangutans have begun to explore on their own.

Beluga Whales

Grown beluga whales mostly make high sounds, while their babies' first sounds are low-frequency. Baby beluga whales learn to make new sounds by copying adults. It takes them a year or more to learn special "contact calls" that help them stay in touch with their mothers.

Aimee Reid is a children's book author who lives in Canada with her husband, three kids, and sweet dog named Sadie, whose adventurous spirit inspires the whole family to try new things.

Sébastien Braun was born in France and studied history at Strasbourg University until he decided to pursue his lifelong calling to study the arts. He started out teaching art until he eventually made the leap to full-time illustrator.